OPUS DEI

The Secrets and Scandals
of an Influential Organisation

Written by François De Heyder
Translated by Jessica Foster

THE SECRETS OF OPUS DEI

KEY INFORMATION

- **Date founded:** 2 October 1928.
- **Official objectives:** to evangelise and to encourage everyone to be holy in their everyday lives.
- **Unstated objectives:** to increase their influence in the Catholic Church, contain the theological change symbolised by the Second Vatican Council and promote the Christianisation of society through political and economic alliances.
- **Most prominent members:**
  - Josemaría Escrivá de Balaguer, Spanish prelate and founder of Opus Dei (1902-1975).
  - Álvaro del Portillo, Spanish prelate, Secretary General of Opus Dei and Escrivá's successor (1914-1994).

INTRODUCTION

Since its creation in 1928, Opus Dei (Latin for 'Work of God', also known as 'the Work') has regularly been the subject of controversy and rumour, particularly due to its secretive nature and the influence it is considered to have, whether or not this is correct, over the Catholic Church and the Pope himself. And for good reason: in the 1950s, according to the regulations of the institution itself, its members were forbidden from revealing that they belonged to the Work without the authorisation of a superior, while a decade earlier they had been advised not to discuss the organisation with non-members. Repeatedly accused of being an elitist and secretive organisation, implicated in various financial and political scandals, Opus Dei certainly stimulates curiosity.

Currently, however, Opus Dei has nearly 90 000 members, which represents only 0.008% of the Catholic population worldwide. While that might seem low, its influence over the Roman Curia is real, whatever its leaders might say. While it is completely detached from the ecclesiastical hierarchy and only depends on the Pope himself, Opus Dei's influence extends far beyond a strictly ecclesiastical setting and reaches the highest economic and political circles.

OPUS DEI THROUGHOUT HISTORY

FOUNDATION OF OPUS DEI

Opus Dei's foundation is closely linked to its founder Josemariá Escrivá de Balaguer, and its development is intertwined with the rise of Francoist Spain (1939-1975).

Portrait of Josemaría Escrivá. This painting can be found in the church of St. Mary of the Angels, Chicago.

Its officially recognised founding date is 2 October 1928, although many believe that the association only properly existed after 1939, the year in which the Spanish Civil War ended and Francisco Franco (1892-1975) came to power. However, when its founder Escrivá was asked about this, he stated that the organisation's beginnings were closely linked to the story of his soul, which is unfortunately a little vague. What we can be sure of nonetheless is that Escrivá agreed to explain subsequently. According to him, in 1928 he had a vision during a retreat in an ecclesiastical residence in Madrid. In this vision, God revealed the project that would later become Opus Dei.

SPAIN IN THE 1930S

Opus Dei's beginnings were humble and peaceful. It more closely resembled a space for reflection and discussion than a body that advocated a strict spiritual withdrawal from the world. The first meetings took place in Madrid in an apartment that Escrivá shared with his family. But the situation soon took a turn. In the 1930s, Spain drastically transformed: it changed regime from a monarchy to a republic, the second republic in Spanish history. After the municipal elections in 1931, the left came to power and the House of Bourbon, represented by King Alfonso XIII (1886-1941), was forced to flee the country.

For the young Escrivá, the 1930s started badly. When the left-wing parties came to power, Spain become brutally secular and anticlericalism spread across the country, particularly in Madrid. Priests were forbidden from teaching, crosses were removed from cemeteries and public buildings, and processions were outlawed. There was total separation between the Church and the state. As the Prime Minister Manuel Azaña (1880-1940) highlighted in a speech before the Cortes on 13 October 1931, "Spain has ceased to be Catholic".

Unhappy with the government and the victory of the Spanish Popular Front in the 1936 elections, the far-right movements united to organise an insurrection and plunged Spain into a civil war. Opus Dei's first members were caught up in the Siege of Madrid and were forced to disperse. They did not meet again until the end of the war in 1939, when Escrivá returned to the capital alongside the Francoist troops. Opus Dei's development only really began again in the early 1940s. At this time it found an important source of support in the Bishop of Madrid, Leopoldo Eijo y Garay (1878-1963). He gave a semblance of official status to the young organisation. In 1941, it acquired the status of 'pious union', according to the Code of Canon Law, but was still not officially recognised by the Holy See.

THE ROMAN PERIOD

Believing that the status granted by Eijo y Garay did not fully portray the organisation's specific nature, Escrivá aimed to adopt a status for it that did not yet exist within canon law. For this reason, he went to Rome in 1946 in order to negotiate the creation of new statuses. However, his tenacity did not initially overcome the inertia in Rome. In fact, Opus Dei did not have enough members and its activities were too marginal for him to be able to hope to be able to influence such an imposing administration. However, a year later, Pope Pius XII (1876-1958) passed a series of texts, including the apostolic constitution *Provida Mater Ecclesia* (1947), which would provide the legal background for the formation of secular institutes. This perfectly corresponded with what Escrivá had been aiming for, and he saw his negotiations conclude successfully.

Arcadio María Larraona Saralegui (1887-1973) was tasked with preparing this constitution. He was helped in this task by two young priests, Álvaro del Portillo and Salvador Canals Navarrete (1920-1975), who were both members of

Opus Dei and were close to Escrivá. The former would take over the leadership of Opus Dei following the death of its founder.

THE SECOND VATICAN COUNCIL

In the years between the adoption of the 'secular institute' status and the Second Vatican Council (1962-1965), Opus Dei's members vastly grew in number, from 3000 to 30 000, including over 300 priests. Escrivá, however, could not hope for any more for his organisation while Pope Pius XII, who had refused to allow Escrivá to become a bishop three times, was still in the Vatican. The election of John XXIII (1881-1963) to the papacy seemed like an opportunity, the objective being to transform the secular institute into a prelate *nullius*.

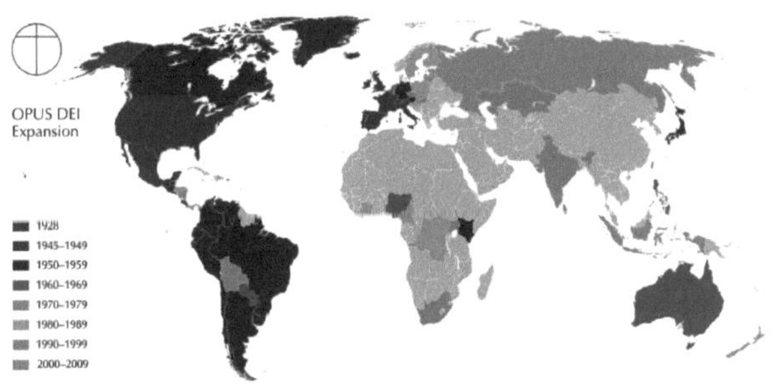

Map showing the expansion of Opus Dei.

The specific nature of Opus Dei meant that it did not cover a distinct geographical area that could fall under the jurisdiction of a diocese: its members were spread throughout the world. Hence Escrivá believed that the status of a prelature that did not fall under the jurisdiction of a diocese, but the authority of the Pope, better suited the organisation's setup. The request was submitted to the Pope in 1960. Two years later, it was refused due to legal and practical difficulties. This was thus another snub to Escrivá who, for the fourth time, had the bishop's mitre denied to him.

A short while later, the Second Vatican Council began. During this council, a proposal aiming to establish a new legal structure that corresponded with Opus Dei's ambitions was going to be debated. However, some considerations caused the organisation to believe that the assembly was going against its principles. Escrivá did not in fact agree to open the assembly to the public and feared that the many experts who had been invited to the debates would eclipse the bishops, who were often less sophisticated and educated. All this helped fuel the resentment that he felt towards John XXIII.

The college of priests and the Chair of Saint Peter, in St. Peter's Basilica, during the Second Vatican Council.

DID YOU KNOW?

Popes are considered to be God's representatives on earth. Within their own churches, however, they rarely create unanimity. John XXIII was no exception. Indeed, Cardinal Giuseppe Siri (1906-1989), who was close to Escrivá and was Pope John's contemporary, described the latter as "the greatest disaster in recent ecclesias-

SCHISMATIC PARANOIA

Pope John XXIII did not live to see the end of his council. His successor, Paul VI (1897-1978) took over and led the discussions to their conclusion. During the assembly, the Pope condemned abortion methods, even though that had not been agreed upon with the bishops. Criticisms therefore poured forth and, among them, Escrivá's voice was heard once again. However, unlike the majority of the people who opposed this condemnation, the latter made it clear that his disagreement was linked to the fact that Paul VI had not taken a strict enough position in his rejection.

His opinions seemed to become more radical the more time passed, and he was now convinced that only Opus Dei could save the Church, which he believed had become too weak and overindulgent. The situation was such that they were close to a schism. The bishop John Roche also stated that the members of Opus Dei were preparing to create their own church, separate from the Catholic Church. However, Álvaro del Portillo, Escrivá's right-hand man, managed to make him see reason and suggested a more diplomatic approach.

A PERSONAL PRELATURE

The years following the council were Escrivá's chance to make his message heard across the world in order to spread Opus Dei's ideas. Completely occupied by his travels, he gave up his work on trying to change Opus Dei's status, which he would never see the completion of. He died in 1975 in Rome and left the leadership of Opus Dei to Álvaro del Portillo. The organisation then entered the last phase of its development to assume the status under which we know it today, that of 'personal prelature'.

Created following the conciliar decree *Presbyterorum Ordinis* (1965), the personal prelature allowed for greater organisational flexibility than existing structures such as dioceses. In 1969, Opus Dei began procedures to reach this status, and in 1982 John Paul II (1920-2005) signed the apostolic constitution *Ut sit*, which finally made it a personal prelature.

DID YOU KNOW?

While the legal structure that allows the creation of personal prelatures has existed since 1965, Opus Dei remains to this day the only organisation to have obtained this status. It is true that it perfectly matches the structure that the organisation had at the time. It would not even by too much of a stretch to think that it was created on account of Escrivá's work.

MOST PROMINENT MEMBERS

JOSEMARÍA ESCRIVÁ DE BALAGUER

Born in 1902 in Barbastro (Aragon, Spain), Escrivá's childhood already attracted astonishment for how miraculous it seemed. Shortly after he was born, he fell victim to a meningitis epidemic that struck the region of Huesca. According to legend, it was only after his mother's pilgrimage to the shrine of Torreciudad that the young Escrivá recovered from his illness. Following economic setbacks, the family fell into poverty and left Barbastro to go to the wine-producing region of La Rioja. An extremely pious child, he was certain from a very young age that his destiny would lead him to serve God.

In 1920, he enrolled at the pontifical university in Zaragoza where, thanks to his excellent results, he was made a 'higher seminarian' in 1922. Three years later, he was ordained a priest and earned a degree in canon and civil law. He eventually moved to Madrid in order to finish his education with a doctorate in law.

Escrivá stated that on 2 October 1928, the feast day of guardian angels, he had a vision during a spiritual retreat in Madrid. This vision was behind the founding of Opus Dei. From that moment onwards, the stories of Escrivá and that of his 'Work' were inextricably linked.

Opinions vary greatly as to Escrivá's personality. One thing is certain: Escrivá was, above all, a man of God. The compassion and devotion that he showed towards his neighbours were an integral part of his being. On the other hand, his bad-tempered, irascible and proud character did him no favours, and influenced Opus Dei's image.

In 1980, five years after his death, the Postulation for the Cause of his beatification introduced the Cause in Rome, following the miraculous recovery of Sister Concepción Boullón Rubio in 1976. Nearly a third of Catholic bishops supported this request and signed the petition. In 1991, the members of the Congregation for the Causes of Saints unanimously confirmed that this was a miracle and therefore granted beatification to Escrivá on 17 May 1992. A year later, another miraculous healing was submitted to be approved by the Congregation, that of Dr Manuel Nevado Rey. It was officially declared to be a miracle in 2001 and, on 6 October 2002, Pope John Paul II canonised Escrivá. This quick canonisation raised many questions, particularly on the subject of the absolute support of the Pope in this procedure.

ÁLVARO DEL PORTILLO

Portrait of Álvaro del Portillo.

Álvaro del Portillo was born in Madrid in 1914 and joined Opus Dei in 1935. Ordained a priest in 1944, he soon earned the trust of the organisation's founder and the position of

Secretary General, which put him in a good position in Opus Dei's setup. He was an extremely important man in Opus Dei's history and his influence was unprecedented. He was notably in charge of the negotiations with the Holy See to obtain a new status for the organisation.

After attending the Second Vatican Council, he held different positions in Rome. He was appointed secretary of the Commission for the Discipline of the Clergy and Christian People and became Consultor for various other commissions, including the Commission for the Discipline of the Faith and the Commission for the Religious.

Thanks to his skills in diplomacy, he managed to moderate Escrivá's obstinacy and ensured that Opus Dei's image was not tarnished by the provocative and at times insensitive tone of its founder. When the latter died, del Portillo assumed leadership of the organisation, before being made a bishop in 1991 by John Paul II. He died in Rome three years later and was declared Venerable by Benedict XVI (born in 1927) in 2012, before being beatified in 2013 by Pope Francis (born in 1936).

AIMS AND FUNCTIONS OF OPUS DEI

HOLINESS IN THE SECULAR WORLD

Opus Dei's main message is fairly simple: any Christian can contribute to spreading Christ's message and take part in the Church's mission of evangelisation without having to withdraw from secular life. The key word was evangelisation through the sanctification of work. Through this message, we can see what is unusual about Opus Dei and understand the difficulties the prelature must have had to overcome to find its way in a Church which had not made space for it. Through this founding idea of holiness in the secular world, Opus Dei made a key distinction between itself and traditional religious orders. Through a simple and active life, Escrivá believed that any Christian could promote traditional Christian values such as humility and patience.

THE ORGANISATION'S STRUCTURE

Opus Dei is managed by three assemblies of decreasing importance. The first is the General Council, which is at the head of the organisation. Specifically, this is a consultative body to which members are nominated for life and whose mission is to direct the organisation. The first prelate of the order was Josemaría Escrivá de Balaguer. He was succeeded by Álvaro del Portillo in 1975, who was in turn replaced in 1994 by Javier Echevarría Rodríguez (born in 1932). The General Council is composed of the prelate, the Vicar General, the Secretary General, three vice-secretaries, a prefect of studies and a general administrator.

Opus Dei's administration is made up of regional councils. Each geographical area with an Opus Dei establishment is divided into regions. These do not necessarily correspond to official state limits. Each of them is directed by a regional vicar who is helped in his task by the regional council as well as by technical councils whose task is above all to ensure that the region's economy is managed well.

Finally, the regions comprise a series of local councils directed by secular leaders, unlike the aforementioned bodies, which are all led by priests.

A HIGHLY STRUCTURED ORGANISATION

Although Opus Dei seems extremely well-structured, Escrivá was not really interested in the matter. When he was asked to explain the Work's structure, he said only that there was a general council in Rome, which itself was reproduced in every country in which the organisation was present. In 1966, he even wrote that Opus Dei was a disorganised organisation. However, two years earlier, Pope Paul VI had praised the organisation's structure, which its leaders prided themselves on.

'WHISTLING', OR JOINING OPUS DEI

To join Opus Dei, it is necessary to have a vocation. Although It is an ecclesiastical organisation, it does not demand any vows similar to those required by traditional religious orders. A layman entering Opus Dei thus remains a layman and his membership is confirmed through a contract. Through this contract, the members commit to support the apostolic action of the organisation and the activities it pursues. In return, the prelature offers support and spiritual training to its new members.

The term 'whistling' means applying to join Opus Dei. Recruitment is generally done at a young age. Sending a letter applying for admission, or 'whistling', can be done from the age of 16 and a half, although it is possible to become a 'candidate' from the age of 14 and a half. However, it is only at the age of 18 that the applicant can make the 'oblation', thus marking their official entry into Opus Dei.

DID YOU KNOW?

Escrivá first used the term 'whistling', as it described the noise of a kettle which, in his opinion, perfectly represented the admission process to Opus Dei. The applicant is made to wait a while, during which time they participate in some of the organisation's various activities in order to acclimatise before definitively joining.

Opus Dei has the reputation of being like a large family in which mutual aid is expected. This also means that when a member decides to quit, he must fully leave and the resentment his former brothers and sisters feel towards him will be intense. This is what happened to one of Escrivá's first collaborators, Miguel Fisac (1913-2006). After leaving the organisation, he decided to get married. His sister, who was still a member of Opus Dei, was sadly not permitted to attend the ceremony. Even worse, when he had just lost one of his children, two Opus Dei representatives who attended the funeral deliberately said within his earshot that this loss was God's punishment for leaving the organisation.

THE MEMBERS OF OPUS DEI

Members are put into different categories: numeraries, supernumeraries, associates and cooperators. This terminology comes from the standards that were used in Spanish university jargon and do not reflect a tendency for occultism.

The supernumeraries, who represent around 70% of all of Opus Dei's members, are generally married members with family obligations. Consequently, they are less available than others to carry out Opus Dei's various activities. Due to their family situation, they do not live alongside their religious brethren in the Opus Dei centres. Moreover, they are still a part of their parish. One of the duties of supernumeraries is to regularly pay money to support the prelature's action.

Numeraries are at the heart of the organisation. They generally consider Opus Dei to be their family. They therefore live in communities in centres that are made available to them. Although, like the other members, they have a profession outside of Opus Dei, many of their day-to-day activities are associated with the institution's interests. Additionally, everything they earn that exceeds the basic minimum they need to live on is paid back to the organisation. Through their spiritual training, which is more advanced than that of the supernumeraries, they are the only ones who are able to carry out key duties within the Work. The priests who are part of Opus Dei are all numeraries and directly answer to the prelate. Their task is essentially to attend to the spiritual needs of the other members, as any man of God would do. Some are also in charge of parishes or university teaching.

The main difference between a numerary and an associate is their place of residence. The associates, who are often celibate, do not live in Opus Dei's centres, generally due to their family responsibilities. As regards everything else, there is no difference between associates and numeraries.

Finally, the cooperators are not members, but 'friends' of Opus Dei, and consequently are not counted in the official figures. Their job is to support the accomplishment of Opus Dei's missions through their activities. Some also occasionally make financial contributions.

OPUS DEI'S ACTIVITIES

Opus Dei's main activity consists of developing community centres and carrying out various activities, the majority of which are linked to education. It has thus been behind the founding of 15 universities. In total, these have over 80 000 students and their faculties include medicine, law, theology, economics, communication, philosophy and the arts. Additionally, Opus Dei is behind 11 business schools with 10 000 students, 36 primary and secondary schools and

97 technical and professional colleges, which teach more than 38 000 pupils. The organisation also has 166 student residences with a total capacity of over 6000 students.

Opus Dei's other main field of work is medicine: the prelature has been responsible for the construction of seven hospitals which together employ over 1000 doctors and 1500 nurses. All these structures are scattered across the world.

CONTROVERSIES

THE MATESA AFFAIR

One of the greatest scandals involving Opus Dei members was the Matesa affair. It had roots in the final years of the Francoist regime and was one of the most notorious cases of corruption in Spain since the end of the civil war.

The textile company Maquinaria Textil del Norte de España Sociedad Anónima was at the centre of the scandal, which broke out in 1969 and concerned the fraudulent acquisition of government funds to export textile machines. The affair quickly sowed doubt regarding the economic reforms implemented in 1959 and the official credit agencies that had been created shortly afterwards. The people behind Spanish economic policy in the 1960s were soon worried. However, it seems that most of them had links with Opus Dei.

The scandal exacerbated tensions between some members of the government who belonged to the Falange (fascist-leaning political party) and the organisation. The former believed that the influence Opus Dei had on the Spanish government had to stop. To this end, the ministers José Ruíz Solís (1913-1990) and Manuel Fraga Iribarne (1922-2012) launched a press campaign against Opus Dei and its technocrats. Although Franco did not feel particularly affected by the scandal, its disclosure and the doubt it cast over the government's credibility drove him to action. As a result, he fired the two ministers, while the members of Opus Dei who had been involved got off lightly. Juan Vilá

Reyes (1925-2007), the director and founder of Matesa who assumed responsibility for the scandal, even received an official pardon from Franco later on.

This scandal was not the only one to involve Opus Dei to a greater or lesser extent. We can notably cite the Ortega Pardo and Meleux affairs, which both involved fraud and had a certain impact during the 1960s.

A CONTROVERSY FROM *THE DA VINCI CODE*

In terms of controversy, it is hard to ignore the outpouring of reactions that followed the 2003 publication of the novel *The Da Vinci Code* by Dan Brown (American writer, born in 1964). The book's preface in fact introduces it as more of a thesis than a fictional novel. This is almost certainly a somewhat provocative literary technique designed to boost sales but, in any case, the novel takes various real and well-known elements alongside others from the author's imagination, which are at best believable but never confirmed, and at worst simply invented. Following the book's success, Opus Dei had to react promptly. The book's content had the potential to offend not only Opus Dei, but Christianity as a whole.

The main objective of the communication plan that the organisation devised consisted of ensuring that the film was unauthorised for minors, then that the film's content was reviewed in order to delete the scenes that could offend Christian sensibilities. Finally, Opus Dei requested that the film be accompanied by a warning specifying that it was a work of fiction. Its second objective was to take advantage of the film's release to openly communicate about the situation of Opus Dei and make its mission known. The first objective was not met, but the second was successful.

OPUS DEI AND THE PAPACY

Opus Dei is nowadays integrated at all levels of the Church, but this has not always been the case. It was only following the election of John Paul II in 1978 that the organisation acquired the political significance that it has today. When he was still the Bishop of Krakow, Karol Wojtyła, to use his real name, was already a friend of Opus Dei and had already benefited from its generosity. During his visits to Rome, for example, he habitually stayed in one of their residences. It is also worth noting that Opus Dei provided financial support to Solidarność ('Solidarity', the Soviet bloc's first independent trade union), an organisation that regularly supported John Paul II.

In 1978, when the conclave gathered in Rome to elect a new pope, Cardinal Wojtyła was Opus Dei's preferred candidate, and the Archbishop of Vienna, who was close to the organisation, tried to use his influence during the election. While John Paul II does not owe his election solely to the support given to him by Opus Dei, he nonetheless did not hasten to return the favour once he was elected. The new status of personal prelature, the quick beatification of Escrivá and the appointment of many Opus Dei members and supporters to positions of close collaboration are perfect examples of this. Moreover, many South American bishops, who were also Opus Dei members, owe their nominations to John

Paul II.

Pope Benedict XVI clearly did not support Opus Dei as openly as his predecessor. Although he was aware of the organisation's sectarianism, he used it to fight against the modern deviances that had appeared within the Church. On the contrary, following Pope Francis's election, the tide turned. His positions are much more progressive than those of his predecessors, and therefore concern traditionalist groups such as Opus Dei.

THE IMPORTANCE OF SECRECY

Opus Dei has always attracted controversy due to its secrecy, both within the Church and elsewhere. It was also the subject of inquiries in the 1930s and 1940s, both in Spain and in Rome. Initially, it was its reputation as 'a form of Christian masonry' that earned it the suspicion of ecclesiastical and political authorities.

As Opus Dei relies on discretion, it is almost impossible to recognise one of its members. This is what many people have problems with.

DID YOU KNOW?

Some theories have gained prominence over time on the basis of certain proven facts. For example, using a particular cologne that Escrivá was especially fond of could indicate that someone belongs to the organisation. A missing cufflink could mean the same thing. The same goes for the greeting of the word 'pax', which is answered with 'in aeternum'. Neither denied nor confirmed by Opus Dei's members, these theories remain speculative.

This desire to be secretive can clearly be seen in the constitution of 1950, in which Escrivá stated the wish to practice 'collective humility', which would make individualism less important. To respect this wish, he therefore advised people not to reveal that they were members of Opus Dei. A more prosaic reason for this imposed secrecy was the Vatican's forbidding members of secular organisations from being involved in its business, which happened in 1950. However, many members of Opus Dei broke this rule, which drove the organisation to tell its members not to identify themselves. In 1982, on the other hand, the statutes of Opus Dei announced a slight relaxation of this rule. Some discretion is still expected, particularly regarding divulging the names of other Opus Dei members, but they are asked to avoid too much sense of mystery, as the organisation officially has nothing to hide. Consequently, its members can act naturally.

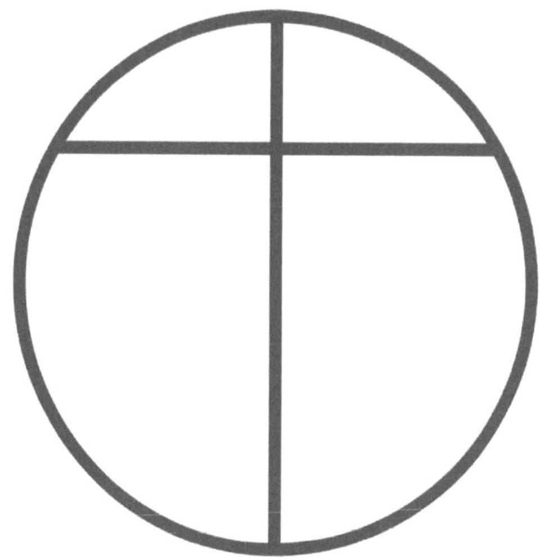

Seal of the Opus Dei prelature.

MORTIFICATION OF THE FLESH

Another element that has contributed to Opus Dei's scandalous reputation is the mortification of the flesh. Under the Francoist regime of the 1940s, a time when Opus Dei was being fiercely attacked, nobody reproached it for this practice. While forms of penitence through mortification were an integral part of Spain's ultra-Christian spirituality, over time, this practice was increasingly considered to be excessive and degrading, to the extent that it fell out of use. Opus Dei, however, remained attached to it, which merely stoked the fire of curiosity that it caused.

The forms of mortification practised by Opus Dei's members vary, but are not intended for everyone. Only celibate members are expected to undergo the most serious forms of mortification, such as the use of a hair shirt or flagellation. A hair shirt is a kind of small chain covered in sharp points that must be worn on the upper thigh or lower back for two hours each day. The whips used in flagellation are in reality small rope knots which the person applies to the back or thighs while reciting a short prayer. In other words, it is often brief and benign. The length of the prayer and the force of the whip are decided by the penitent.

Less serious and therefore more ordinary mortifications also exist. For example, it is common to make sleeping uncomfortable sometimes. This may involve doing without a pillow, sleeping on the floor or lying on a plank. In the same way, some members choose to observe a silence that begins after the evening meal and lasts until the next day.

Finally, such practices match the state that Opus Dei is in today: it is an organisation that is strongly attached to the past, refuses to evolve and stands firm against the innovative ideas that Pope Francis now represents.

SUMMARY

- Opus Dei was founded by Josemaría Escrivá de Balaguer in 1928. Closely linked to the personal story of its founder, it was created in Francoist Spain.
- After its quiet beginnings, the situation of Opus Dei was turned upside down at around the same time as that of Spain. With the country's brutal secularisation, clergy members were hunted down and Escrivá was forced to leave Madrid.
- In 1941, Opus Dei acquired the status of a pious union and, in 1947, that of a secular institute, a status that had just been created by Pope Pius XII.
- Following the Second Vatican Council, the founding father became more radical in his viewpoint, meaning that the positions of Opus Dei also became more radical. Del Portillo's intervention was the only thing that prevented Opus Dei from completely disassociating itself from the Catholic Church.
- When its founder died, Opus Dei entered a new stage of its development, aimed at obtaining the status of a personal prelature, which it successfully achieved in 1982.
- The fundamental principle that governs the lives of Opus Dei's members is that of the secular mission. Through work and everyday life, members can reach holiness.
- The prelature's structure is made up of three hierarchical levels. The first and most important is the General Council, presided over by the prelate, the head of Opus Dei. The second is that of the regional councils, which are directed by a regional curate. The third is composed of

local councils, directed by laypersons.

- Currently, Opus Dei has over 90 000 members. This number includes 2000 priests, the rest being laypersons. Most members are supernumeraries, while numeraries can probably be considered to be the most dedicated to the activities of Opus Dei.
- Opus Dei's area of expertise is education. It has therefore been responsible for the creation of 15 universities, 11 business schools, 36 primary and secondary schools and 97 technical and vocational colleges. Its other area of expertise is medicine: it has founded seven hospitals.
- The main subject of controversy is Opus Dei's secretive nature. The wish to undertake 'collective humility' led the organisation to create internal rules that forbade its members from revealing that they belonged to Opus Dei. In fact, the prelature now believes that joining such an organisation is a personal matter and therefore requires discretion rather than secrecy.

We want to hear from you!
Leave a comment on your online library
and share your favourite books on social media!

FIND OUT MORE

BIBLIOGRAPHY

- Allen, J. L. (2005) *Opus Dei: An Objective Look Behind the Myths and Reality of the Most Controversial Force in the Catholic Church*. New York: Doubleday.
- Beevor, A. (2006) *The Battle for Spain: The Spanish Civil War 1936-1939*. New York: Penguin Books.
- Cahill, T. (2008) *Pope John XXIII: A Life*. London: Penguin Books.
- Hertel, P. (1998) *Les secrets de l'Opus Dei. Enquête et documents*. Villeurbanne: Golias.
- Hutchinson, R. (2006) *Their Kingdom Come: Inside the Secret World of Opus Dei*. London: St. Martin's Press.
- Le Vaillant, Y. (1971) *Sainte Maffia : le dossier de l'Opus Dei*. Paris: Mercure de France.

ADDITIONAL SOURCES

- Brown, D. (2006) *The Da Vinci Code*. New York: Anchor.
- Del Carmen Tapia, M. (2006) *Inside Opus Dei: The True, Unfinished Story*. New York: Bloomsbury Academic.
- Escrivá, J. (2006) *The Way: The Essential Classic of Opus Dei's Founder*. New York: Doubleday.
- Walsh, M. (2004) *Opus Dei: An Investigation into the Powerful Secretive Society Within the Catholic Church*. London: HarperCollins.

ICONOGRAPHIC SOURCES

- Portrait of Josemaría Escrivá. This painting can be found in the church of St. Mary of the Angels, Chicago. Royalty-free reproduction picture.
- Map showing the expansion of Opus Dei. Royalty-free reproduction picture.
- The college of priests and the Chair of Saint Peter, in St. Peter's Basilica, during the Second Vatican Council. © Lothar Wolleh.
- Portrait of Álvaro del Portillo. Royalty-free reproduction picture.
- Seal of the Opus Dei prelature. Royalty-free reproduction picture.

FILMS AND DOCUMENTARIES

- *Decoding Opus Dei.* (2006) [Documentary]. George Tzimopoulous. Dir. USA: Great Projects Film Company Inc.
- *The Da Vinci Code.* (2006) [Film]. Ron Howard. Dir. USA: Columbia Pictures.
- *There Be Dragons.* (2011) [Film]. Roland Joffé. Dir. Spain: Antena 3 Films.

IMPROVE YOUR GENERAL KNOWLEDGE

IN A BLINK OF AN EYE !

www.50minutes.com